FUN Skills

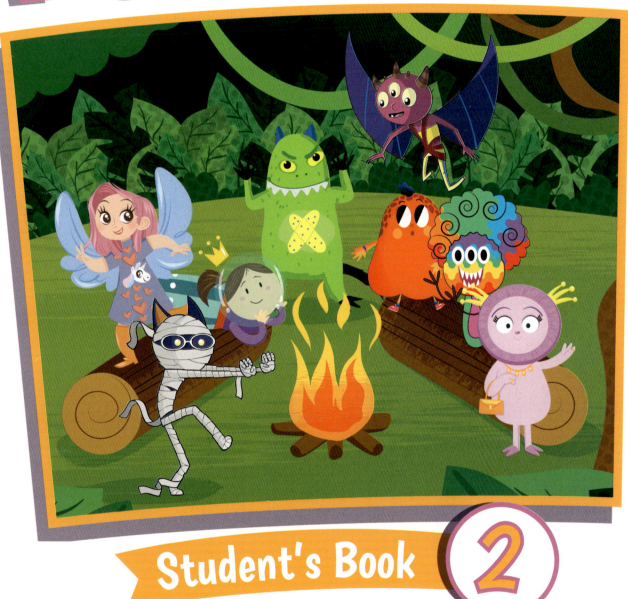

Student's Book 2

Claire Medwell • Montse Watkin

Cambridge University Press
www.cambridge.org/elt

Cambridge Assessment English
www.cambridgeenglish.org

Information on this title: www.cambridge.org/9781108673013

© Cambridge University Press and Cambridge Assessment 2020

This publication is in copyright. Subject to statutory exception
and to the provisions of relevant collective licensing agreements,
no reproduction of any part may take place without the written
permission of Cambridge University Press.

First published 2020

20 19 18 17 16 15 14 13 12 11 10 9 8

Printed in Poland by Opolgraf

A catalogue record for this publication is available from the British Library

ISBN 978-1-108-67301-3 Student's Book and Home Booklet with Online Activities

The publishers have no responsibility for the persistence or accuracy
of URLs for external or third-party internet websites referred to in this publication,
and do not guarantee that any content on such websites is, or will remain,
accurate or appropriate. Information regarding prices, travel timetables, and other
factual information given in this work is correct at the time of first printing but
the publishers do not guarantee the accuracy of such information thereafter.

Contents

Map of the book		4
1	My school bag	6
2	Fun in the park!	10
	Review 1–2	14
3	It's my birthday!	16
4	My favourite things	20
	Review 3–4	24
5	Let's go shopping!	26
6	Cool homes	30
	Review 5–6	34
7	What would you like?	36
8	Let's have fun!	40
	Review 7–8	44
9	Let's go to the zoo!	46
10	Fun on the beach	50
	Review 9–10	54
11	Our things	56
12	What's your favourite game?	60
	Review 11–12	64
Pairwork		66
Grammar fun!		70
Grammar fun pairwork!		76
Skills checklists		78
Word list		82
Meet the characters		86
Acknowledgements		88

Map of the book

Unit	Topic	Skills focus	Can do	
1 My school bag page 6	School bags and contents	**Reading and Writing** Read short sentences and recognise key words Tick or cross to show if a sentence is true or false	Read and understand short, simple words and the names of familiar objects	Chant Think Big
2 Fun in the park! page 10	Leisure activities	**Reading and Writing** Read short sentences about a picture and say whether they are true or not	Understand basic descriptions of everyday activities	
Review Units 1–2 page 14				
3 It's my birthday! page 16	Birthday activities Prepositions of place	**Listening** Identify key words in descriptions of people and select the correct name for each person by drawing a line to connect them **Speaking** Give and respond to simple instructions using prepositions of place	Understand simple spoken descriptions Understand and follow spoken instructions to point at and place objects in a picture	Chant
4 My favourite things page 20	Favourite things	**Reading and Writing** Spell simple words correctly **Speaking** Respond to simple questions	Unjumble words to match a picture Answer questions with simple answers and respond to *Tell me about …* questions	Chant
Review Units 3–4 page 24				
5 Let's go shopping! page 26	Things you can buy	**Listening** Listen for and write numbers (1–20) Spell names	Understand and write letters of the alphabet when heard Understand and write numbers 1–20 when heard	Song Think Big
6 Cool homes page 30	Houses, rooms and furniture	**Reading and Writing** Read a text, then choose and copy words to complete sentences	Understand and copy simple words	Think Big
Review Units 5–6 page 34				

Unit	Topic	Skills focus	Can do	
7 What would you like? page 36	Food	**Speaking** Understand and respond to personal questions	Understand simple questions Give simple answers	Chant
8 Let's have fun! page 40	Pastimes and hobbies	**Listening** Listen for specific information Tick the correct box under a picture	Understand simple spoken descriptions of people and everyday objects	Think Big
Review Units 7–8 *page 44*				
9 Let's go to the zoo! page 46	Animals	**Reading and Writing** Read questions about a picture story Write one-word answers	Answer simple questions about a picture	Song Think Big
10 Fun on the beach page 50	Seaside activities	**Listening** Listen to words, colours and prepositions Locate objects and colour them correctly	Understand and follow simple basic instructions Follow a short story in simple English	
Review Units 9–10 *page 54*				
11 Our things page 56	Personal possessions	**Speaking** Understand and answer questions about pictures of objects	Understand simple questions Give simple answers	Song
12 What's your favourite game? page 60	Games	**Reading and Writing** Read short sentences about a picture and say whether they are true or not.	Can understand basic descriptions.	Chant
Review Units 11–12 *page 64*				

Pairwork *pages 66–69*
Grammar fun! *pages 70–75*
Grammar fun pairwork! *pages 76–77*
Skills checklists *pages 78–81*
Word list *pages 82–85*
Meet the characters *pages 86–87*

1 My school bag

1. 💬 **Look at the photos. Talk with a friend.**

   1 How many school bags can you see?
   2 What colours are they?
   3 What colour is your school bag?

2. 🔊 02 **Listen and match the bags to the children.**

1 Eva 2 Sue 3 Ben 4 Tom

THINK BIG
Which bags are good?

❸ 💬 **Look at Max's school bag. How many things can you name?**

Max's bag

My bag

❹ ✏️ **Draw three objects in your bag and write.**

I've got _____ , _____

and _____ in my school bag.

❺ 💬 **Find out about your friend's bag.**

What's in your bag?

I've got a ruler.

Me too!

❻ 👁 **Read, think and write.**

1 ✓ It's in Max's bag. ✗ It's not in my bag.
It's _____ .

2 ✓ It's in my bag. ✗ It's not in Max's bag.
It's _____ .

3 ✗ It's not in my bag. ✗ It's not in Max's bag.
It's _____ .

It's a notebook!

1 💬 **Look at the photos. Talk with a friend.**

What's this? | What are these? | It's a/an ... | They're ...

Let's tidy up!

2 🎵 03 **Listen to the chant and match the photos.**

3 ✏️ **Complete the words.**

Example post _e_ _r_
1 _ _ _ _ board
2 book _ _ _ _ _
3 _ _ _ _ puter
4 key _ _ _ _ _

4 💬 **Work with a friend. Give instructions and tidy your classroom.**

> **TIP!**
> Don't forget to say *please* and *thank you*!

5 👁 **Look and read. Put a tick (✓) or a cross (✗) in the box. There are two examples.**

Examples

 This is a pen. ✓    These are rulers. ✗

Questions

1  These are desks. ☐

2  This is a cupboard. ☐

3  This is a bookcase. ☐

4  These are crayons. ☐

5  This is a poster. ☐

2 Fun in the park!

1. 💬 **Look at the park for 30 seconds. What can you see?**

2. 👁 **Cover the picture and work with a friend. How many questions can you answer?**

   1 What colour are the bikes?
   2 What animals are there?
   3 How many children are there?
   4 Where is the kite?
   5 What sports can you see?
   6 What's in the water?
   7 What has the monkey got?
   8 What is Frankie eating?

3. 🎧 04 **Listen and circle the word you hear.**

   1 see (bee)
   2 sun fun
   3 bike kite
   4 boat boots
   5 dogs ducks
   6 bat bag

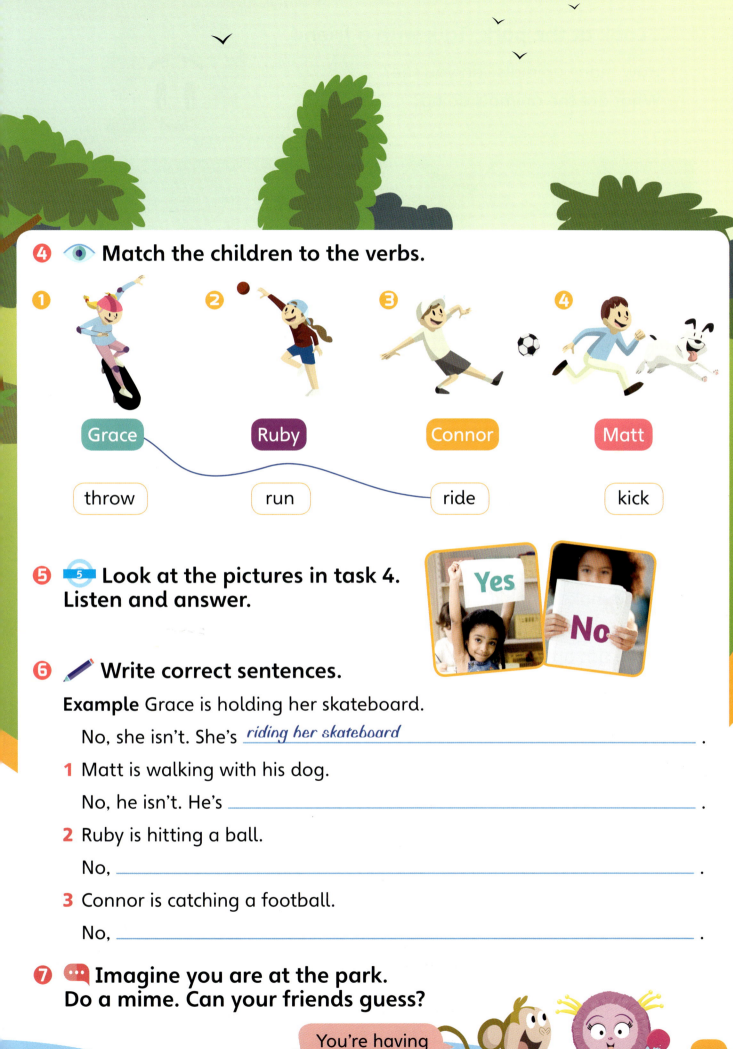

1 💬 **Look at the park. Talk with a friend.**
   1 How many animals can you see?
   2 What are the animals doing?

2 👁 **Look and read. Write *yes* or *no*.**

Example A girl is walking with her dog. ___yes___
   1 The snake is holding an ice cream. _____
   2 The crocodile is riding a bike. _____
   3 The fish are sleeping in the water. _____
   4 Grandpa has got a camera. _____
   5 The monkey is flying a kite. _____

3 ✏ **What's in the photos? Find and write the words.**

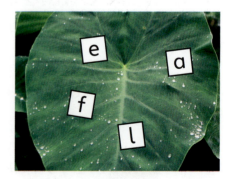

1 f _ _ _   2 _ _ _ _ _ _   3 _ _ _ _

4 👁 Read and choose the correct words.

Enjoy a dirty / clean park.
Throw / Don't throw your rubbish in the bin!

5 💬 What is good? Choose the correct picture.

A   B   C

6 👁 Read the signs and match to the children in task 5. Write A, B or C.

① ☐ Don't walk on the flowers.

② ☐ Don't throw rubbish in the park.

③ ☐ BE NICE TO ANIMALS.

7 ✏ Make a word tree! Look at page 66.

Review Unit 1

Skills: Speaking, Writing and Reading

1 Talk with a friend. Look at the photo and answer the questions.

1 Where are the children?
2 Name four things you see in this classroom.
3 Name four things you don't see.

Mark: ___ / 9

2 Look at the photos and write the words.

Eva

Ben

Sue

1 Eva's bag is ___orange___ . It's in the _____ .
2 Ben's bag is _____ . It's on the _____ .
3 Sue's bag is _____ . It's next to the _____ .

Mark: ___ / 5

3 Read and draw the things.

Example
   a football in the bookcase
1 a computer on the desk
2 a mouse next to the computer
3 a ruler in the school bag
4 a clock on the bookcase
5 three crayons on the chair

Mark: ___ / 5
Total: ___ ___ / 19

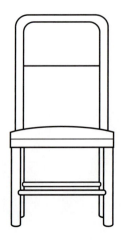
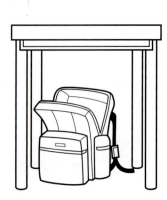

Review Unit 2

Skills: Reading and Writing

1 Look at the photos. Write these words on the lines.

~~hit~~   kick   ride   run

   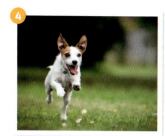

1. hit
2. _____
3. _____
4. _____

Mark: ___ / 3

2 Look at the pictures and read the sentences. Write A or B.

1 A girl is riding a bike. A
2 A boy is catching a basketball. ___
3 A teacher is running. ___
4 Two ducks are swimming. ___

5 A dog is jumping. ___
6 A girl is throwing a toy. ___
7 A boy is flying a kite. ___
8 A girl is kicking a football. ___

Mark: ___ / 7

3 Look at the colours and write Frankie's sentences.

1 | ball | window. | Don't | the | next to | the | kick |

Don't _____ _____ _____ _____ _____ .

2 | your | on | Don't | bike | grass. | ride | the |

_____ _____ _____ _____ _____ _____ .

Mark: ___ / 6
Total: ___ ___ / 16

3 It's my birthday!

Who is not sharing?

1 👁 **Read and point to the photos.**
- A get a special card
- B open presents
- C play party games
- D wear new clothes
- E sing a song
- F eat special food

2 💬 **Talk with two friends. What do you do on your birthday?**

I wear new clothes. So do I! I don't!

3 ✏️ Can you guess what the presents are? Write the words.

1. k _i_ _t_ _e_
2. b _ _ _ _
3. r _ _ _ _ _
4. t _ _ _ _ _
   b _ _ _ _
5. l _ _ _ _
6. b _ _ _

4 🚇06 Where are the presents? Listen and draw lines.

5 💬 Draw a toy on a small sticky note. Look at the picture in task 3. Give instructions to your friend.

Put the robot in front of the chair!

between | under | next to | behind | in front of

1 🔊 07 **Listen to the chant and draw lines.**

2 🔊 08 **Listen and circle the correct words.**

1 **She's** / **Her** name's Sara. **She's** / **Her** nine years old.
2 **He's** / **His** name's Dan. **He's** / **His** seven years old.

3 💬 **Ask and answer with a friend.**

- How old are you?
- What's her name?
- How old is he?

4 ✏️ **Draw and write about you and your friend.**

❺ 💬 **Look at the picture of a birthday party. What can you see?**

❻ 🔊 **Listen and draw lines. There is one example.**

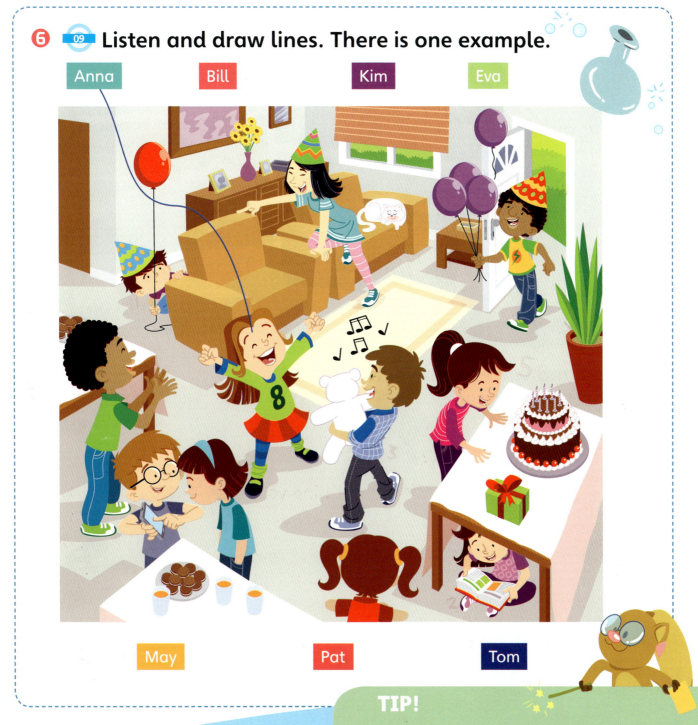

TIP!
There is one extra name. What is it?

❼ 👁 **Make a pop-up birthday card! Look at page 67.**

4 My favourite things

1. 🔟 **Find and write Nedda's favourite things. Then listen and check.**

My favourite …
colour rhymes with **new**. _blue_
animal rhymes with **frog**. _____
toy rhymes with **white**. _____
food rhymes with **snake**. _____
place rhymes with **tree**. _____

2. 👁 **Read the groups of words. Circle the word that is not correct.**

1 colour	2 animal	3 toy	4 food	5 place
brown	giraffe	bread	pea	pink
(bear)	goat	board game	pear	park
black	grapes	ball	paper	playground

3. 💬 **Ask a friend about their favourite things.**

What's your favourite colour?

It's blue.

> **TIP!** Use only the letters in the hearts.

4 ✏️ Look at the pictures.
Look at the letters. Write the words.

Example

  _m a n g o_

Questions

1  _____

2   _____

3   _____

4  _____

5  _____

5 👁️ Read and draw.

1 sweets on the cake
2 five peas on the ice cream
3 lemon in the lemonade
4 a monster in the story book

6 🎵 Listen to the chant. Draw the faces in task 5.

 = like    = don't like

21

❶ ✏️ **Look and write the words. Write one more question.**

	Me	My friend

1 Do you like p _ _ _ _ _ _ _ _ _ on your pizza?

2 Do you like big s _ _ _ _ _ _ at the zoo?

3 Do you like s _ _ _ under your feet?

4 Do you like f _ _ _ _ _ _ _ on TV?

5 _____?

Yes, I do! = 🙂   No, I don't! = ☹️

❷ 💬 **Ask and answer with a friend. Draw the faces in task 1.**

❸ 💬 **Talk about the picture with a friend. Take turns to ask.**

1 What's this?
2 Where is the alien?
3 What colour are the alien's eyes?
4 How many birds are there?
5 What is the alien doing?
6 Tell me about the lizard.

TIP! It's OK to say: *Sorry, I don't understand. Can you say that again, please?*

4 🔊 **Listen to the interview and circle the correct information.**

1 The alien **likes / doesn't like** monsters.
2 The alien **likes / doesn't like** the sun.
3 Its favourite food is peas on **pizza / ice cream**.
4 The alien's favourite hobby is **flying / painting**.
5 It **likes / doesn't like** pink.

5 ✏️ **Draw and write about an alien.**

My alien's name is _____ .

My alien has got _____

_____ .

My alien lives _____

_____ .

My alien likes _____

_____ .

My alien doesn't like _____

_____ .

6 💬 **Show your alien to your friends.**

My alien's name is Zak.

What a cool alien!

Thanks!

What beautiful colours!

Review Unit 3

Skills: Speaking, Writing and Reading

1 Look at the photos and talk with a friend. What can you see? What are the children doing?

Mark: ___ / 4

2 Read the text. Write these words on the lines.

games   He   Her   ~~my~~   eight   too

Hi, I'm Sam! This is ____my____ friend, Bill. Bill is six years old. **1** _____ has got a sister. **2** _____ name is Suzi. She's **3** _____ years old. On Bill's birthday, we play **4** _____ and eat cake. We sing Happy Birthday! Bill likes birthdays. Me **5** _____ !

Mark: ___ / 5

3 Look at the picture. Choose the correct word.

Example The car is **in front of** / (**next to**) the robot.

1 The teddy bear is **next to** / **on** the table.
2 The cakes are **next to** / **in front of** the teddy bear.
3 The boy is **between** / **behind** the girls.
4 The toys are **under** / **on** the table.
5 The cat is **between** / **behind** the guitar.

Mark: ___ / 5

Total: ___ ___ / 14

24

Review Unit 4

Skills: Listening, Writing and Reading

1 🔊 13 What are Lucy's favourite things? Listen and circle.

A  B  C  D

E  F  G  H

Mark: ___ / 4

2 ✏️ Now write about Nick.

1 Nick's favourite animals are _l i z a r d s_ and _____ .

2 Nick doesn't like pizza. His favourite food is a  _____ .

3 His favourite place is the _____ .

4 Nick has a red _____ . He plays with it in the park.

5 What is Nick's favourite colour? Yes, that's right, it's _____ .

Mark: ___ / 5

3 Look at the picture and read the questions. Circle the correct answer.

Example What animal is in the sea?	(a fish) / a lizard	
1 What colour is the bird in the tree?	green / purple	
2 How many children are there?	two / three	
3 What is the boy wearing?	boots / a hat	
4 What is he holding?	a boat / a fish	Mark: ___ / 5
5 What is the girl doing?	jumping / swimming	Total: ___ ___ / 14

5 Let's go shopping!

1. 💬 Talk with a friend. Name the things in the trolleys. Ask and answer.
   — Some crayons. — Trolley A!

2. ✏️ Look at the trolley on page 68 for 30 seconds. Then write the words.

   1 _____   3 _____   5 _____
   2 _____   4 _____

3. 🎧 14 Listen and tick (✓) the letter you hear.

   1 t ☐   d ☐   2 p ☐   b ☐   3 a ☐   h ☐   4 i ☐   y ☐
   5 f ☐   s ☐   6 g ☐   j ☐   7 m ☐   n ☐   8 b ☐   v ☐

4 ✏️ Write the first letters. Are the letters the same as in task 3?

 _d_ olls

 __ ineapples

 __ ats

 __ ce cream

 __ ish

 __ eans

 __ eatballs

 __ oots

5 💬 Student A: Look at task 4. Ask three questions.
Student B: Close your book and write.

> Can you spell …?

> How do you spell …?

6 🔊 15 Listen and write the surnames.

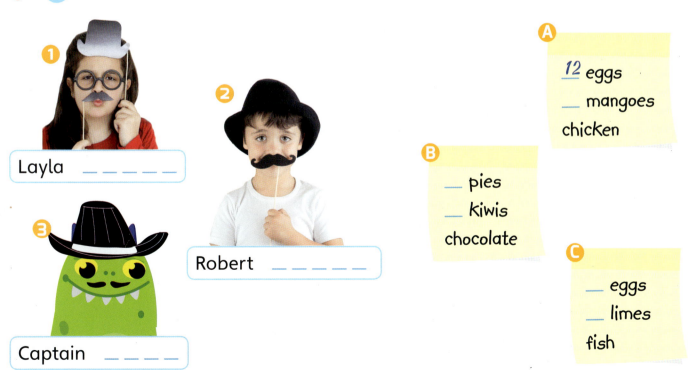

7 🔊 15 Listen again. Match the people to the shopping lists. Write the numbers in the shopping lists.

① 🎵 **Listen to the song and do the maths. How many sunflowers are in the flower shop?**

| 20 | − | 5 | = | ☐ | | ☐ | − | ☐ | = | ☐ |

| 15 | − | ☐ | = | ☐ | | ☐ | − | ☐ | = | ☐ |

② ✏️ **Complete your shopping list. Draw and write.**

w _ _ _ _ _ _ _ _ _

_ _ _ _ _ _ _ _ _ _

_ _ _ _ _ _ _ _ _ _

p _ _ _ _ _ _ _

t _ _ _ _ _ _ _ _

_ _ _ _ _ _ _ _ _ _

③ 💬 **Play with a friend. Who can buy the things first?**

> I'd like a watermelon, please.

> Here you are.

> Can I have three tomatoes, please?

28

④ ✏️ **Read and point. Write the words.**

We see numbers:
1 on a _ _ _ _ _ _ in our classroom. (k o c c l)
2 in a clothes _ _ _ _ _ . (h o s p)
3 on a _ _ _ in the street. (s u b)
4 on a birthday _ _ _ _ . (c e a k)
5 on the _ _ _ _ of a house. (o d o r)

THINK BIG
Where do you see numbers?

⑤ 👁 **Read the questions in task 6. Say *name* or *number*.**

⑥ 🚇17 **Read the question. Listen and write a name or a number. There are two examples.**

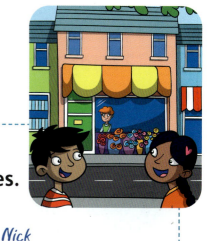

Examples

| What is the boy's name? | *Nick* |
| How old is he? | 9 |

Questions

1 What is the name of the street?   _____ Street
2 What number is the shop?   _____
3 Who is in the shop?   Mrs _____
4 How many flowers does the girl want?   _____
5 Who are the flowers for?   _____

TIP!
All the answers are names or numbers.

6 Cool homes

❶ ✏️ **Write the questions. Ask a friend.**

1 do where live you?
___ ___ ___ ___?

2 rooms many are how there?
___ ___ ___ ___ ___?

❷ 💬 **Imagine you live in this tree house.**

1 What's good about your tree house?
2 What's bad about your tree house?
3 What animals live in the tree with you?
4 What furniture is in your tree house?

❸ **Draw some furniture in your tree house. Talk about it with a friend.**

There is a big armchair.

There are lamps.

30

4 ✏️ **Can you complete the sentences? Read and write your ideas.**

I live in a **1** _____ near my school.

There is a big kitchen, a dining room, a bathroom and three **2** _____ .

In my bedroom, there is a white cupboard with my **3** _____ . I've got a brown box with lots of **4** _____ . On the wall, there's a mirror and a poster of my favourite animal. It's an **5** _____ .

My ideas:
1 _____
2 _____
3 _____
4 _____
5 _____

5 🔊18 **Are your ideas correct? Listen and write the words in task 4.**

6 🔊19 **Listen and point. Tell a friend what jobs you can see.**

7 🔊20 **Listen and match. Who's speaking?**

1 Finn — A I make my bed.
2 Cara — B I put my toys in the toy box.
3 Luke — C I put things on the table for dinner.
4 Molly — D I clean the kitchen floor.

THINK BIG
What jobs do you do at home?

1 💬 Talk with a friend.
What can you see?

Molly's bedroom

Finn's bedroom

Cara's bedroom

2 ✏️ Read about Molly. Look and write about Finn and Cara.

> Molly's favourite animal is the polar bear. She likes animals.
> She loves reading.

1 Finn plays the _____
 and the _____ . He loves playing with _____ .

2 Cara's favourite colours are _____ and _____ .
 She plays _____ . She likes _____ .

3 ✏️ Look at page 68. Draw three things in your bedroom.
What do we learn about you?

My favourite _____ is
_____ .
I like _____ .
I love _____ .

④ 👁 Read this. Choose a word from the box. Write the correct word next to numbers 1–5. There is one example.

> **TIP!**
> Cover the pictures. Can you guess the missing words?

Frogs

Do you like frogs? They are fantastic and cool! Frogs have four ___legs___ - two are long and two are short. Many frogs are green but some are grey or yellow. I like to sleep at **1** _____ but they like to sleep in the morning. Some people have a **2** _____ for a pet, but I have a frog! My frog doesn't live in my bathroom or under my **3** _____ . It lives in water in my **4** _____ . And my frog does not close its **5** _____ even when it sleeps! I love my frog!

Example
legs | night | garden | eyes
bed | apple | kite | dog

⑤ 💬 Choose words to describe these houses. Which house do / don't you like?

A   B   C

> beautiful and scary   funny and silly   fantastic and cool

⑥ Draw a house. Show your house to your class and talk about it.

> This is my house!

> It's fantastic and cool!

Review Unit 5

Skills: Reading, Listening and Writing

1 Look at the people in the shops. Read and write the word.

I would like some ___flowers___, please.

Can I have that red 1 _____, please?

Here you are. A bag of 2 _____.

Would you like a 3 _____?

Can I have some new 4 _____?

Mark: ___ / 4

2 🚇 21 Listen and write the number.

Mark: ___ / 5

3 Read the questions. Choose and write the answers.

1 How old is Pat? _____
2 Who is your teacher? _____
3 How many kiwis would you like? _____
4 How do you spell your name? _____
5 What number is your house? _____

> Seven, please.
> W-E-B-B.
> Mr Brown.
> 8 years old.
> It's 15.

Mark: ___ / 5

Total: ___ ___ / 14

Review Unit 6

Skills: Reading, Writing and Speaking

1. **Look at the house and number the rooms 1–5.**

   Example living room ___Room 5___

   1 kitchen _____   3 dining room _____
   2 bedroom _____   4 bathroom _____

   Mark: ___ / 4

2. **Look at the house. Where are the people? Read the sentences and write the room.**

   Example Tom is sitting on the sofa. He's in the ___living room___.

   1 Grace is cleaning the cupboards. She's in the _____.
   2 Alex is putting things on the table for dinner. He's in the _____.
   3 Lucy is making the bed. She's in the _____.
   4 Mark is in the bath. He's in the _____.

   Mark: ___ / 4

3. **Look at the photo. Imagine this is your bedroom. Write the words on the lines.**

   My bedroom has got a big w _i_ _n_ _d_ _o_ _w_. My
   1 d _ _ _ is in front of the window. I haven't got a
   computer. There is a big 2 b _ _ _ _ _ _ _ _ with lots
   of books. It's next to my 3 b _ _ _. My bedroom is very
   clean. All my 4 t _ _ _ _ are in boxes.

   Mark: ___ / 4

4. **What's in your bedroom? Say two sentences to a friend.**

   Mark: ___ / 4
   Total: ___ ___ / 16

7 What would you like?

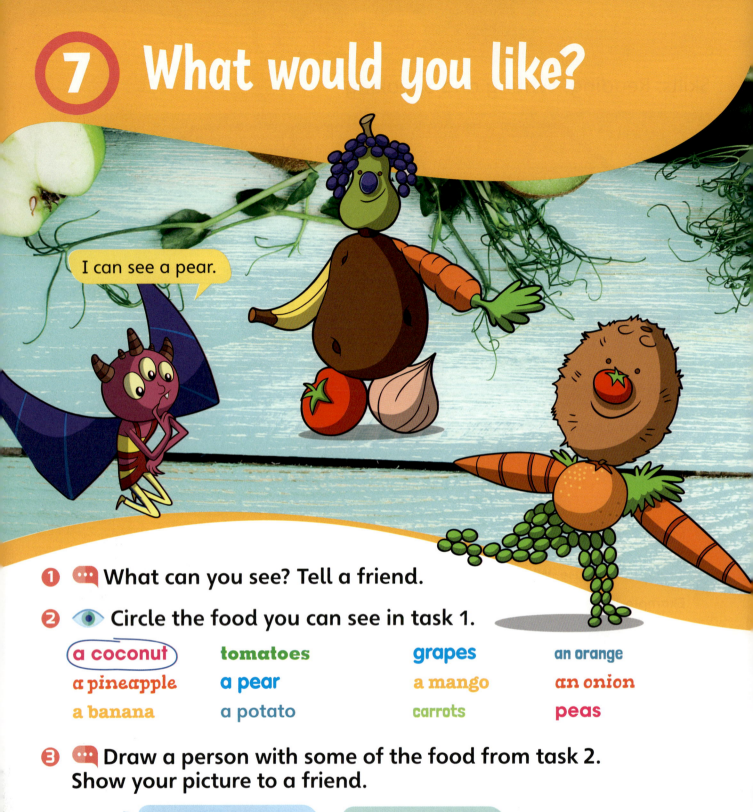

I can see a pear.

1 💬 What can you see? Tell a friend.

2 👁 Circle the food you can see in task 1.

(a coconut)	tomatoes	grapes	an orange
a pineapple	a pear	a mango	an onion
a banana	a potato	carrots	peas

3 💬 Draw a person with some of the food from task 2. Show your picture to a friend.

Look at my picture.   I can see grapes.

4 🚇22 Listen to the chant and say the letters. Then listen and write.

 1 l _ _ _ _ _ _ _

 2 o _ _ _ _ _ _ _

 3 c _ _ _ _ _ _ _

 4 t _ _ _ _ _ _ _

5 🔊 23 **Making a cake! Listen and put a tick (✓) or cross (✗). Write the number.**

	✓ / ✗	Number
bananas	✓	4
kiwis		
carrots		
eggs		
mango		
lemon		
orange		

6 👁 **Read and ask a friend.**

This is my favourite fruit. Do you know its name? Can you see a star? It's a star fruit!

This is my favourite fruit. It's a very big fruit. It's a jackfruit. I like eating it with rice and coconut.

1 Do you want to eat a starfruit?
2 Would you like to eat a jackfruit?

 Yes!   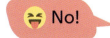 No!   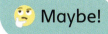 Maybe!

7 ✏️ **Draw a picture and write about your favourite fruit.**

This is my favourite fruit.
It's _____ .
I like eating it with _____ .

37

1 💬 **Ask and answer with a friend.**

What's this?   It's …

What are these?   They're …

2 🔊 **Listen and number the pictures.**

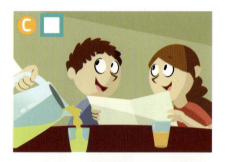

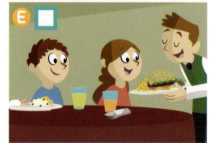

3 🔊 **Listen and repeat.**

This is the menu.

What would you like?   I'd like orange juice, please.

I'd like chicken with rice, please.

Here you are.   Mmm … thank you!

4 ✏️ Write a menu.

5 💬 Work in groups of three. Imagine you are in a café. Act out.

I'd like an ice cream, please.

Here you are.

6 Ask and answer with a friend.

What's your favourite fruit / drink / lunch?

Do you like … ?

8 Let's have fun!

1. She's _____ .
2. They're _____ .
3. He's _____ .
4. They're _____ .

❶ 💬 Talk with a friend. What's missing in each picture?

❷ ✏️ What are the children doing? Choose and write the words in task 1.

> dancing   drawing a picture   flying a plane   painting a picture
> playing badminton   playing the drums   playing the guitar   singing

❸ 🔊 26 Listen to Tom and circle the correct answers.

Example
His favourite class at school is **doing sport** / **painting**.

1 His teacher is **Mrs Green** / **Mrs White**. She's really cool!
2 He likes painting **people** / **animals**.
3 Today, he's **drawing** / **painting** a cat in class.
4 His picture is **not good** / **fantastic**!

4 💬 Write a question. Interview two friends.

Name	_____	_____
What's your favourite sport?	_____	_____
What do you like painting?	_____	_____
Do you like singing?	_____	_____
Do you like _____ ?	_____	_____

5 Talk to your class about your friends.   *Ben likes playing tennis.*

6 Talk with a friend. What can you see in the pictures in task 7?

7 🔊 27 Listen and tick (✓) the box. There is one example.

What is Sam painting?

A ☐   B ☐   C ✓

3 What is Matt taking a photo of?

A ☐   B ☐   C ☐

1 What is Anna taking to school?

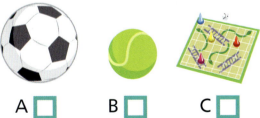

A ☐   B ☐   C ☐

4 What does Grace play?

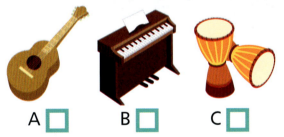

A ☐   B ☐   C ☐

2 What sport is Alice playing?

A ☐   B ☐   C ☐

5 Which painting is Mark looking at?

A ☐   B ☐   C ☐

1 💬 **Look at the painting for one minute. Close your book. How many things can you remember?**

> There's a bed, a chair …

2 ✏️ **Write these words on the lines.**

> behind   between   next to   ~~on~~   under

Example There are five pictures ___on___ the wall.

1 There's a chair _____ the table and the bed.
2 There's a table _____ the mirror.
3 There's a picture _____ the window.
4 There are clothes _____ the bed.

THINK BIG

Three of these paintings are by a very famous artist. Can you find out his name?

3 **Which paintings do you like? Choose words and write.**

> scary   funny   silly   beautiful   cool   fantastic

It's _____ .

It's _____ .

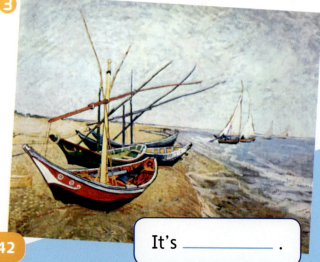

It's _____ .

It's _____ .

42

④ 💬 **Talk to your friends about the paintings in task 3.**

> I like painting 2.

> Me too! It's beautiful!

> I don't! I like painting 1.

⑤ ✏️ **Look at painting 1 again. Read and write *yes* or *no*.**

Example The man is playing a guitar.   *yes*
1 There are a lot of people behind the man.   _____
2 The women have got fruit in their hair.   _____
3 The man is wearing a baseball cap.   _____
4 The man is singing.   _____

⑥ **Choose and write words about painting 3.**

> beautiful   boats   ~~cloudy~~   green   painting   sand

It's a ___*cloudy*___ day. There are four **1** _____ boats on the
2 _____ . There is a red one, a **3** _____ one and two blue ones.
Some more **4** _____ are sailing on the sea. I like this **5** _____ .

⑦ 👁 **Play a game with a friend.**

You need a dice.
1 Play in pairs.
2 Roll the dice.
3 Look at the number.
4 Colour part of the cat's body.

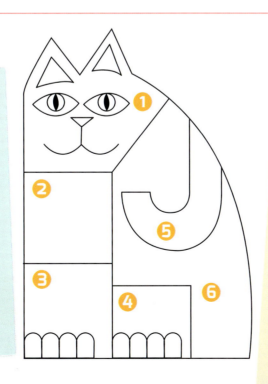

1 🎲 Colour the cat's head green.
2 🎲 Colour the cat's body yellow.
3 🎲 Colour the cat's big foot red.
4 🎲 Colour the cat's small foot blue.
5 🎲 Colour the cat's tail purple.
6 🎲 Colour the cat's back orange.

43

Review Unit 7

Skills: Listening, Writing and Speaking

1. 🔊 28 **Whose lunch is it? Listen and match. Write A, B or C.**

   Mark: ___ / 3

   egg   1 _____   2 _____   3 _____   4 _____   5 _____

2. **What food can you see? Write on the lines in task 1.**

   Mark: ___ / 5

3. **Which food do you like? Ask your partner two questions.**

   Do you like …?   What's your favourite …?

   Mark: ___ / 4

4. **Read the questions. Number the answers.**

   1. Do you like bananas?
   2. Would you like a drink?
   3. What would you like?
   4. Here you are!

   Mmm … thank you! ☐
   Yes, please. I'd like lemonade. ☐
   I'd like a burger, please. ☐
   Yes, I do. They're my favourite fruit. 1

   Mark: ___ / 3
   Total: ___ / 15

Review Unit 8

Skills: Writing and Reading

1 What does Lucy like doing at school? Write these words.

doing sport   taking photos   ~~painting~~   playing the piano   singing

painting

1 _____

2 _____

3 _____

4 _____

Mark: ___ / 4

2 Look at Lucy's painting. Write *yes* or *no*.

Example There's a bed under the window. _yes_   3 There's a cat on the bed. _____
1 There are some pictures on the wall. _____   4 There's a door next to the desk. _____
2 There's a bookcase next to the bed. _____   5 There's a rug in front of the bed. _____

Mark: ___ / 5

3 Answer the questions about Lucy's painting.

1 How many pictures are there?   There are _____.
2 Do you like the painting?   Yes, I _____. / No, I _____.
                                     It's _____.

Mark: ___ / 3
Total: ___ ___ / 12

45

9 Let's go to the zoo!

I think it's a tiger.

1 💬 **Which animal is it? Talk with a friend and write the numbers.**

bird ☐ elephant ☐ hippo ☐
lizard ☐ tiger ☐ zebra ☐

2 ✏️ **Read and colour.**
1 red
2 yellow
3 black
4 white

3 👁 **Look at the photos and choose the correct words.**
1 I'm a **polar bear** / **hippo**.
2 I'm **white** / **grey**.
3 I've got **big** / **small** teeth.
4 I eat **birds** / **fish**.
5 I live in a **cold** / **hot** place.
6 I can **fly** / **swim**.

4 ✏ **Look at the photos and write.**
1 I'm a _____.
2 I'm _____.
3 I've got _____.
4 I eat _____.
5 I live _____.
6 I can _____.

THINK BIG
Some crocodiles are 5 metres long! How long is 5 metres? Find out!

5 💬 **Student A: Think of an animal. Student B: Ask three yes/no questions.**

Does it live in … ?
Does it eat … ?

Has it got … ?

Can it … ?

Is it … ?
Is it a … ?

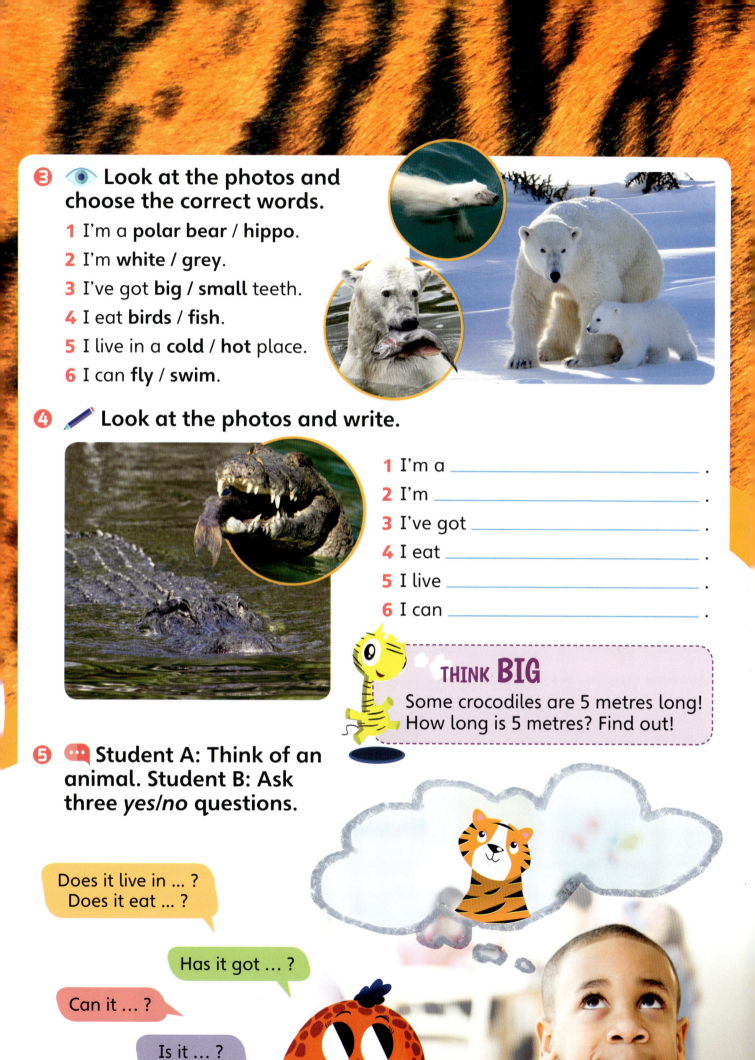

1 🔊 29 **Listen to the song and number the pictures.**

2 👁 **Answer the questions. Draw lines.**

1 Which animal is climbing a tree?
2 What is the giraffe doing?
3 Where is the tiger?
4 What is the tiger doing?
5 Which animal is throwing water?

A It's eating leaves.
B It's under the tree.
C the monkey
D the elephant
E It's sleeping.

3 🔊 29 **Which of these words are in the song? Tick (✓) the words.**

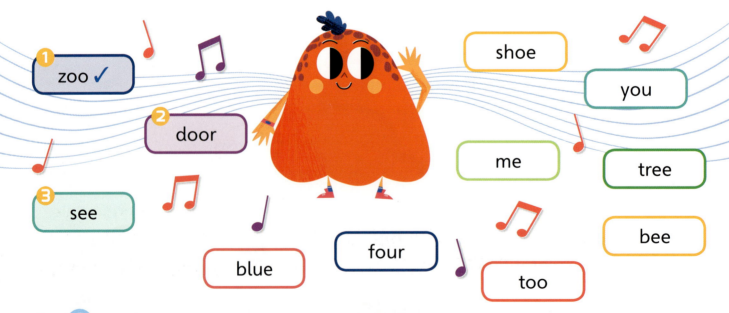

1 zoo ✓
2 door
3 see
blue
four
shoe
you
me
tree
bee
too

4 🔊 30 **How do the eight words sound? Put the words in groups 1–3. Then listen and check.**

48

5 💬 **Look at the pictures in task 6. What can you see?**

6 👁 **Read the questions. Write one-word answers.**

Examples

Where are the animals? in the ____zoo____

How many animals are there? ____five____

1 What is the boy looking at?

a _____

2 Where is the balloon?

in the _____

3 What is the monkey standing on?

the _____

4 Who has got the balloon now?

the _____

5 Is the boy sad?

no, he's _____

7 💬 **Talk with a friend. Who helps the boy? Who can you help?**

TIP! Write only **one** word in your answers.

I can _____ .

10 Fun on the beach

1. 🔊 31 **Close your eyes and listen to four sounds. Then open your eyes and tick (✓).**

2. ✏️ **Look at the photos in task 1 and write the words.**

1 ___sea___
2 _____
3 _____
4 _____

5 _____
6 _____
7 _____
8 _____

3 💬 **Look at the photos in task 1. Answer with a friend.**
1 Which things do you play with on the beach?
2 Which things can you see on the beach?
3 Which things do you find in the sea?

4 **Talk with a friend. What do you like doing at the beach?**

I like running on the beach.   So do I!

I like playing tennis.   I don't!

5 🔊 32 **Listen and colour. There is one example.**

TIP! Learn the names of the colours.

1 👁 **Look at the pictures and tick (✓) the things on each list.**

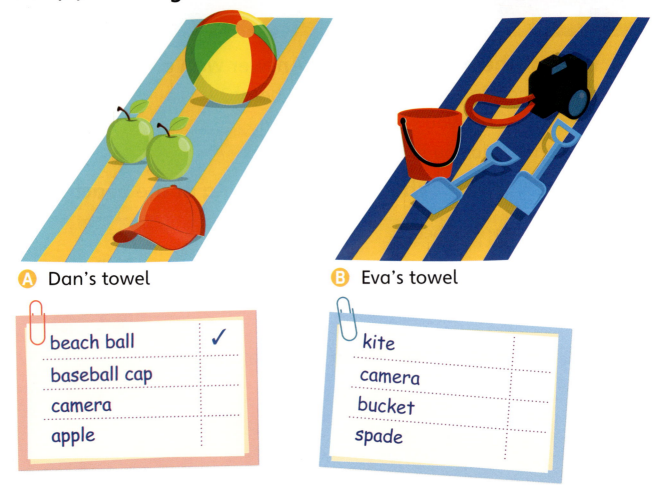

A Dan's towel

beach ball	✓
baseball cap	
camera	
apple	

B Eva's towel

kite	
camera	
bucket	
spade	

2 ✏️ **Write sentences about Dan and Eva.**

Example Dan's got a _beach ball_ .
1 Dan's got two _____ .
2 Dan hasn't got a _____ .
3 Eva's got _____ .
4 Eva _____ .

3 💬 **What do you take to the beach? Draw and show a friend.**

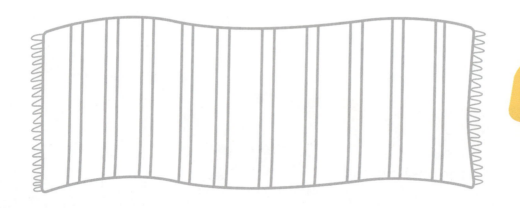

I've got …

4 🔊 33 **What does Dan like doing? Listen and tick (✓).**

5 🔊 33 **Listen again. Circle *yes* or *no*.**

Example Dan likes flying a kite.   yes / (no)
1 He plays tennis with his sister.   yes / no
2 He's got a camera.   yes / no
3 He doesn't like making sandcastles.   yes / no

6 👁 **Make a sandcastle with Sam! Choose and write the words.**

   put   ~~draw~~   make   find   take

Draw a circle in the sand.

3 _____ shells on the beach.

1 _____ sand in the bucket with a spade.

4 _____ a photo of your fantastic sandcastle!

2 _____ a big sandcastle!

Sam sees shells on the sandcastle!

7 🔊 34 **What does Piper say? Listen and repeat.**

Review Unit 9

Skills: Reading, Listening and Writing

1 Look at the picture. Read and write *yes* or *no*.

Example A monkey is eating a banana in the tree. ____yes____

1 Two hippos are swimming in the water. _____
2 A zebra is running behind the tiger. _____
3 An elephant is standing in the water. _____
4 A giraffe is sitting next to the elephant. _____
5 A bear is catching a fish from the water. _____

Mark: ___ / 5

2 🔊 35 Which animal is it? Listen and number the animals in the picture.

Mark: ___ / 6

3 What are the animals doing in the picture? Write five sentences in your notebook.

Example *The elephant is throwing water.*

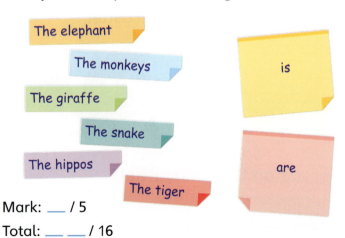

eating the tree.
swimming in the water.
playing in the tree.
running.
throwing water.
sleeping under the tree.

Mark: ___ / 5
Total: ___ ___ / 16

Review Unit 10

Skills: Speaking, Writing and Reading

1 Look at the beach and talk with a friend. What are the children doing?

> Look! A girl is swimming.

Mark: ___ / 6

2 Write the names of the things in the picture.

1 b <u>o</u> <u>a</u> <u>t</u>
2 j __ __ __ __ __ __ __
3 f __ __ __
4 s __ __
5 s __ __ __ __ __ __ __ __ __
6 c __ __ __ __ __ __

Mark: ___ / 5

3 Read and draw the missing things in the picture.

1 A boy is flying a kite.
2 A girl is taking a photo of a bird.
3 A woman is eating an ice cream.
4 Two children are playing with a ball.
5 There are two shells on the sand.
6 There is a ship on the sea.

Mark: ___ / 6

Total: ___ ___ / 17

11 Our things

Jade   Tom   Sara

1 **Look at the picture. Answer the questions.**
1 How many children can you see?   2 What are the children doing?

2 🔊36 **Listen to the song. Is the picture in task 1 correct?**

3 👁 **Whose are the things? Look, read and choose.**

Examples It's **Sara's** / (**Jade's**) watch.   2 It's a bag. It's **hers** / **his**.

📱 It's a phone. It's (**hers**) / **his**.   3 It's **Sara's** / **Jade's** baseball cap.

1 👓 They're **Tom's** / **Jade's** glasses.   4 🧥 It's a jacket. It's **hers** / **his**.

4 🔊37 **Listen and circle the words with the /ɪz/ sound.**

 watch**es**   camera**s**   sunglass**es**   hors**es**   baseball cap**s**   sandwich**es**

5 🚌 38 **What can you see in the photos? Listen and number.**

What a cool school trip!

6 👁 **Match the sentences to the photos. Write A–F.**
1 We're walking in the forest. ___
2 We're listening to our teacher. _A_
3 She's eating her lunch. ___
4 We're giving food to the goats. ___
5 We're standing next to the school bus. ___
6 He's looking at the flowers. ___

7 💬 **Talk with a friend. Where do you like going on school trips?**

I like this.   So do I. It's fun!   I don't! It's scary!

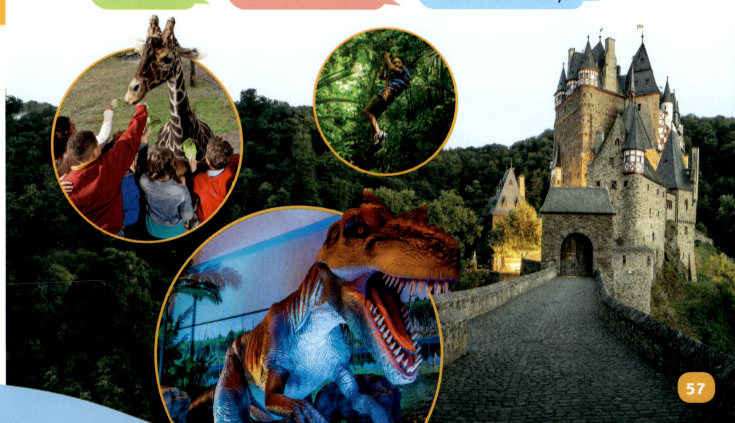

1 👁 **What's missing? Read and draw in the desks.**

Hi I'm Diego! This is my desk. There are two **rulers**, some **pencils** and my favourite blue **baseball cap**. I've got a **painting** of this lovely butterfly!

Hello everyone! I'm Joel. There are lots of things in my desk. I have three **books**, a red **baseball cap**, **a tablet** and a **ball**.

Hello, I'm Hana. This is my desk. It's my favourite colour – red. I have a **book** to read, a yellow **baseball cap**, my **glasses** and this beautiful paper **ball**!

2 💬 **Point to the things in the desks. Ask and answer.**

Whose is this?   It's Diego's.

3 ✏️ **Whose is this? Write *mine* or *yours*.**

1. It's _mine_.
2. It's _yours_.
3. It's _____.
4. They're _____.

4 Draw four of your things. Ask and answer with a friend.

What's this?

Whose is this?

What colour is it?

5 Work in groups. Read the instructions and play a game!

1 Sit in a circle. Put your pictures on the floor.

2 Choose a picture.

3 Ask and answer.

Is this yours?

Yes, it is!

12 What's your favourite game?

1 ✏️ Look and write the words.

1. m <u>o u s e</u>
2. k _ _ _ _ _ _ _ d
3. w _ b _ _ _ _
4. t _ b _ _ _
5. g _ _ _ _
6. c _ _ _ _ _ _ _ _

2 💬 Look and talk with a friend. What are the children doing? Do you like these games?

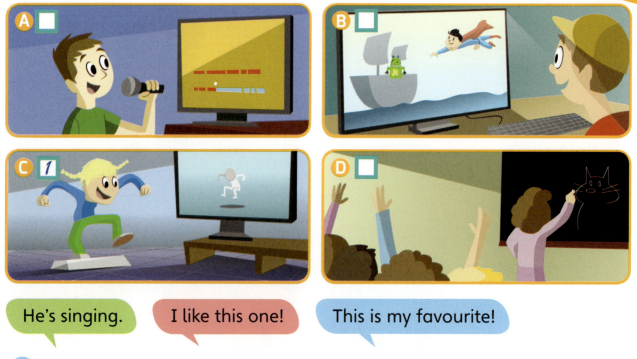

He's singing.   I like this one!   This is my favourite!

3 🔊 39 Listen and number the pictures in task 2.

4 👁 **Look and read. Write *yes* or *no*.**

Examples

The girl is holding her tablet. _____no_____

There are four people in the room. _____yes_____

Questions

1 There is an armchair next to the door. _____
2 The man has got the mouse in his hand. _____
3 The boy is singing. _____
4 The woman is looking at her tablet. _____
5 The dog is behind the sofa. _____

5 🎧 40 **Listen and clap. Then say the chant.**

Websites are fun!
Tablets are cool!
Computers are fantastic,
But playing tennis rules!

6 ✏ **Write your own chant.**

_____ FUN!

_____ COOL!

_____ FANTASTIC,

But _____ !

1. 💬 **Look at the photos and talk with a friend. What are the children doing?**

THINK BIG

Which pictures show good ideas?

2. 🔊 41 **Listen and check your ideas. Which of these things do you do?**

3. ✏️ **Choose words and write.**

choose ~~open~~ play read write

Open the app.

_____ your name.

_____ about the game.

_____ a character.

_____ the game!

4 👁 **Look at the picture and answer the questions.**

Example What's the character's name?
1 What colour are his clothes?
2 What can he do?
3 Where does he live?
4 Where is he going?

His name is _Captain Zoom_ . His clothes are green and
1 _____ . He can 2 _____ . He lives in a big
3 _____ . He's going to the 4 _____ in the sea.

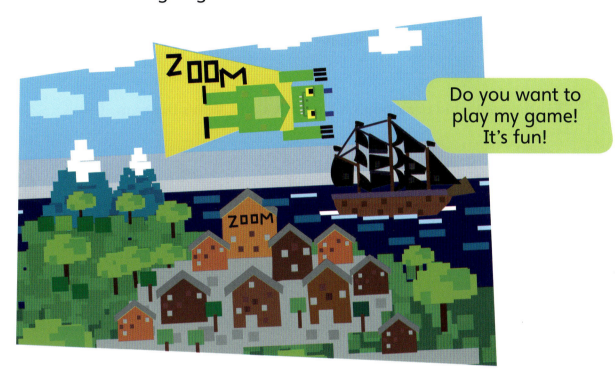

5 ✏ **Make a computer game character! Think about the questions and make notes. Then look at page 69.**

1 What is your character's name?   _____
2 What does it wear?   _____
3 What can it do?   _____
4 Where does it live?   _____

6 💬 **Show your game to a friend and talk about it.**

Review Unit 11

Skills: Listening, Writing and Reading

1 🚇 42 **What do Ann and Matt like doing? Listen and tick (✓) the photos.**

Mark: ___ / 4

2 🚇 42 **Listen again and circle Ann's things in red and Matt's things in green.**

Mark: ___ / 5

3 Answer the question.

Whose is the blue baseball cap?   Whose is the red baseball cap?
It's __Matt's__ / It's __his__ .   It's _____ / It's _____ .

Mark: ___ / 2

4 Match the questions and answers.

1 Do you like my photos?   A In the country.
2 Is this your camera?   B Yes, they're cool!
3 Where do the children live?   C Ssshh! I'm listening to the teacher!
4 How many children are there?   D No. They're Tom's.
5 Are these your books?   E Yes, it is. It's mine.
6 What are you doing?   F There are two.

Mark: ___ / 5
Total: ___ ___ / 16

Review Unit 12

Skills: Reading and Writing

1 Choose the words and write.

> tablet　　keyboard　　mouse　　~~website~~　　phone

I **look at** the _website_ .　　I **read** on my _____ .　　I **write** on the _____ .

I **choose** with the _____ .　　I **listen** to music on my _____ .

Mark: ___ / 4

2 Look at the game and choose the answers.

Example What's the character's name?
It's *Captain Zoom* / *Jesse.*

1 What colour are her clothes?
They're **beautiful** / **blue and pink**.

2 Where is she?
She's **under the sea** / **on the beach**.

3 What can she do?
She can **run** / **swim**.

4 Where is she going?
She's going to **the shell** / **boat**.

Mark: ___ / 4

3 Answer the questions.

1 What's your name?　_____

2 What are you wearing?　_____

3 Where do you live?　_____

4 What's your favourite game?　_____

Mark: ___ / 8

Total: ___ ___ / 16

Pairwork

Unit 2 page 13

7 Make a word tree!

1 Find leaves in the park.

2 Put the leaves under paper and rub with a crayon.

3 Cut out the leaves.

4 Write your favourite park words on your leaves.

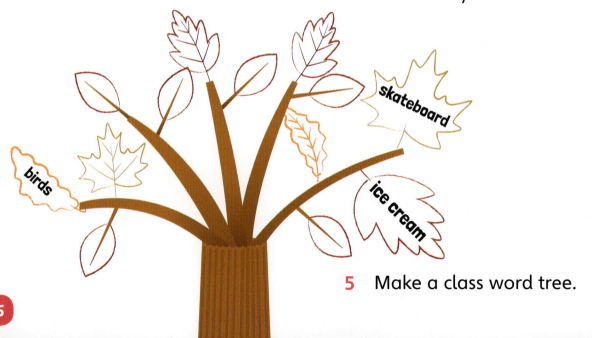

5 Make a class word tree.

Pairwork

Unit 3 page 19

7 **Make a pop-up birthday card!**

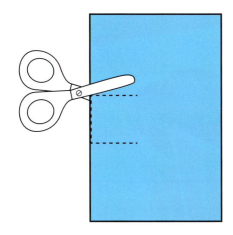

1 Fold and cut your card.

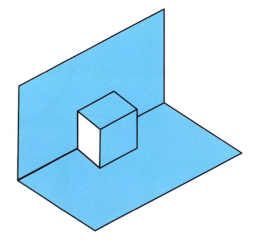

2 Open the card to make the box.

3 Draw your birthday picture.

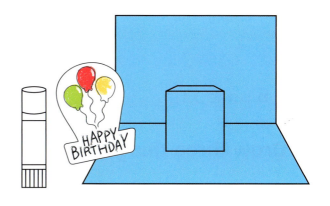

4 Stick your picture on the box.

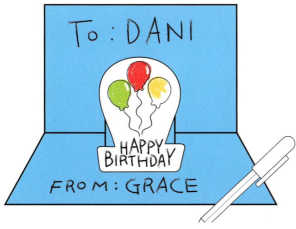

5 Write your card.

6 Give your card to a friend.

Pairwork

Unit 5 page 26

2 Look at the trolley. How many things can you remember in 30 seconds?

Unit 6 page 32

3 Draw three things in your bedroom.

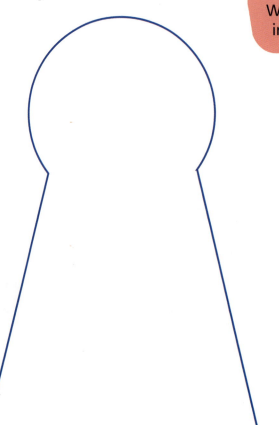

What can you see in my bedroom?

Pairwork

Unit 12 page 63

❺ Make a computer game character! Draw and write.

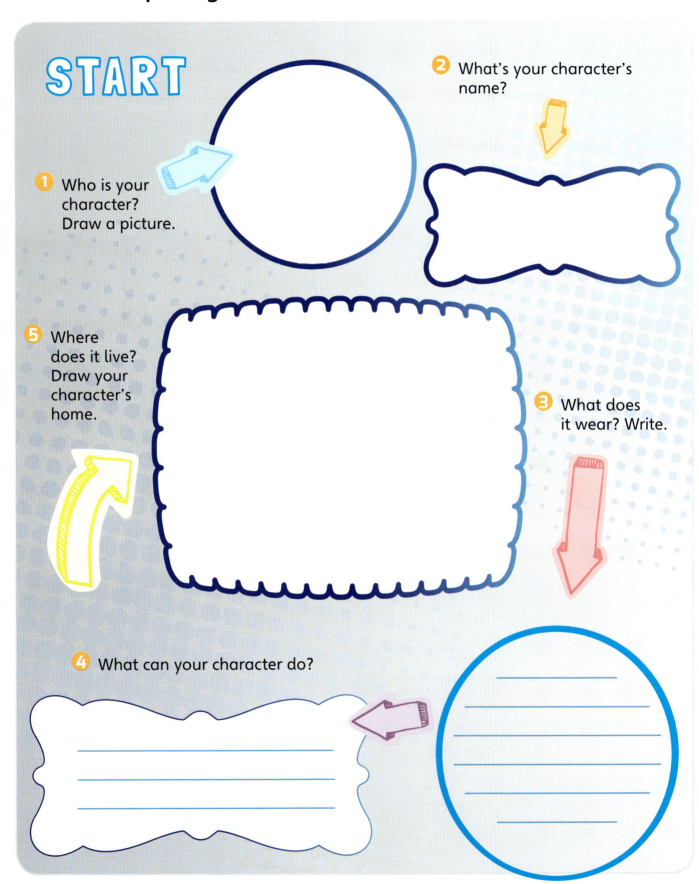

Grammar fun!

Unit 1

○ Question words *what*, *how*, *who*, *how many*

What colour is your bag?
What's in your bag?
What do you do at school?
How do you go to school?
How many students are in your class?
Who's your best friend?

what's = what is
who's = who is

1 Write the question words.

1 A: _____ have you got on your desk?
   B: A book, a pencil and a ruler.

2 A: _____ is that boy?
   B: It's Hugo.

3 A: _____ chocolates are there?
   B: Ten!

4 A: _____ do you learn English?
   B: I go to classes and read books.

○ *Have got* for possession

What **have** you **got** in your bag?	
Have you **got** a pen?	Yes, I **have**. / No, I **haven't**.
She **has got** / She**'s got** a cat. She **hasn't got** a dog.	

2 Complete the sentences. Use *have got*.

1 What _____ you _____ in your bedroom?

2 Ben _____ a teddy bear called Fred.

3 Q: _____ you _____ a helicopter?
   A: Yes, I _____ .

4 Q: _____ she _____ a pet?
   A: No, she _____ .

Unit 2

○ Imperatives

Walk on the grass.	**Don't walk** on the grass.
Eat your lunch.	**Don't eat** your lunch.

1 Match the sentences to the pictures.

1 Enjoy your food! _____
2 Be quiet! _____
3 Sleep well. _____
4 Close the window. _____

A

B

C

D

2 Complete the sentences with a verb from the box.

drink   smile   go   show   draw   ~~bounce~~

Example   *Don't bounce* the ball. (✗)

1 I'm tired. _____ to sleep! (✓)

2 _____ in my book. (✗)

3 Let's take a photo. _____ ! (✓)

4 _____ that juice. It's mine. (✗)

5 _____ me your drawing. (✓)

Grammar fun!

Unit 3

○ Question word *where*

> **Where** are the presents?
> **Where** do you meet your friends?

1 Match the questions to the answers.

1 Where does Tom sit?
2 Where do they live?
3 Where does Mark sleep?
4 Where is Sue?

A In a big bed.
B In the playground.
C In an apartment.
D At the front of the classroom.

○ Prepositions of place (*on*, *under*, *next to*, *in front of*, *behind*, *between*)

> There's a teddy bear **on** the chair.
> The mouse is **under** the sofa.
> The sweets are **next to** the chocolates.
> The bike is **in front of** the house.
> The ball is **behind** the dog.
> The monster is **between** the table and the balloons.

2 Write the prepositions.

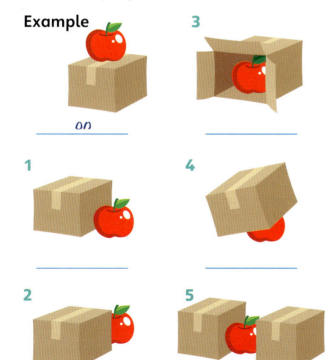

Unit 4

○ What (*a/an/–*) + adjective + noun

> What **a** cool alien!
> What **an** angry robot!
> What fantastic shoes!

1 Complete the sentences with
What a/an/– **and the adjective.**

1 _____ pineapple! (nice)
2 _____ hats! (beautiful)
3 _____ hippo! (old)
4 _____ room! (clean)
5 _____ feet! (big)
6 _____ monster! (ugly)
7 _____ film! (scary)
8 _____ clothes! (cool)

Grammar fun!

Unit 5

○ Determiners *a*, *the*, *some*

> I've got **a** book.
> I've got **an** apple.
> I've got **some** books and **some** apples.
> What's the name of the street?

1 Choose the correct answers.
1. I've got **a** / **an** pet.
2. She's got **a** / **an** elephant.
3. They've got **a** / **an** question.
4. We've got **a** / **an** motorbike.
5. He's got **a** / **an** orange.
6. You've got **a** / **an** computer.

2 Complete the sentences with *a*, *an*, *the* or *some*.
1. Have you got _____ pen?
2. _____ ball under the chair is red.
3. There are _____ monkeys in the tree.
4. I want _____ apple.
5. I want _____ grapes.
6. _____ bus at school is green.

Unit 6

○ Present simple questions with *do* and short answers (*Yes, I do / No, I don't*)

Do you **like** frogs?	Yes, I **do**. / No, I **don't**.
Does she/he/the monster **make** her/his/its bed?	Yes, she/he/it **does**. / No, she/he/it **doesn't**.
Do they **clean** the floor?	Yes, they **do**. / No, they **don't**.

1 Put the questions in the correct order.
1. you / do / badminton? / play
   _____
2. like / she / music? / does
   _____
3. clean / does / he / bedroom? / his
   _____
4. photos? / do / take / you
   _____

2 Write questions.

Example (the robot / sing songs)
Does the robot sing songs?

1. (Abdullah / like pizza)
   _____
2. (Lucy and Kim / read many books)
   _____
3. (you / know the answer)
   _____

3 Answer the questions.
1. Do you walk to school?
   _____ (✓)
2. Does the monster eat bananas?
   _____ (✗)
3. Do Sofia and Matt like cheese?
   _____ (✗)

Grammar fun!

Unit 7

Would like + noun or verb

I'd like a drink.	
She'd like to eat a starfruit.	
Would you like to eat a jackfruit?	Yes, I would. / No, I wouldn't.

I'd = I would
She'd = She would

1 Complete the sentences with *would like* and the noun or verb.

1. Anna _____ . (an apple)
2. Nick _____ . (eat chilli)
3. Matteo _____ . (some new trousers)
4. Eva and Sam _____ . (swim in the sea)
5. _____ you _____ ? (come to my house)
6. _____ Ben _____ ? (a sandwich)

2 Answer the questions.

1. Would you like a drink?
   _____ (✗)
2. Would you like to take a picture?
   _____ (✓)
3. Would Lucy like to play?
   _____ (✓)

Unit 8

Adverbs: *really, very*

This painting is **very** famous.
She's **really** cool!

1 Put the sentences in the correct order.

1. doll / beautiful. / is / really / that
   _____
2. dirty. / is / bike / my / very
   _____
3. really / this / burger / good. / is
   _____
4. hair / long. / is / very / my
   _____
5. spiders / cool. / really / are
   _____

2 Add *very* or *really* to the sentences.

1. This watermelon is nice.
   _____
2. My skateboard is old.
   _____
3. That monkey is silly.
   _____
4. The jellyfish is scary.
   _____
5. My bedroom is clean.
   _____

73

Grammar fun!

Unit 9

○ *Can* for ability

> **Can** you see?
> I **can** understand English.
> I **can't** see without my glasses.

1 Match the sentences to the pictures.

1 The baby can wave. ☐
2 She can't sing. ☐
3 He can play the guitar. ☐
4 He can't carry the suitcase. ☐
5 They can read Chinese. ☐

A

B  C

D

E

Unit 10

○ Nouns: countable and uncountable

> **Countable**
> Dan's got a beach ball.
> Eva's got two spades.
> **Uncountable**
> Would you like **some water / rice / milk**?
> Would you like to listen to **some music**?
> **Irregular**
> There are three **fish** in the sea!
> There are two **people / men / women / mice / children**.
> Cats have four **feet**.

1 Look and write. Use a number for countable nouns and *some* for uncountable nouns.

1 *some rice*

2 *two apples*

3 _____

4 _____

5 _____

○ *Can* for requests/permission

> **Can** I **colour** the jellyfish?
> **Can** I **have** some birthday cake?

2 Put the sentences in the correct order.

1 throw / ball? / the / I / can
   _____

2 some / have / water? / can / I
   _____

3 question? / ask / I / can / a
   _____

Grammar fun!

Unit 11

○ Possessive pronouns *mine*, *yours*, *his*, *hers*, *ours*, *theirs*

| Whose watch is it? | It's my watch. = It's **mine**.
It's your watch. = It's **yours**.
It's his watch. = It's **his**.
It's her watch. = It's **hers**.
It's our watch. = It's **ours**.
It's their watch. = It's **theirs**. |

1 Complete the sentences with the correct possessive pronoun.

1 Is that robot _____ ? (you)
2 This is _____ ! (me)
3 That's not my classroom, it's _____ . (they)
4 I like my hat but I love _____ . (she)
5 This puppy is _____ . (we)
6 Those cats are _____ . (he)

2 Choose the correct answers.

1 I love your drawing. Do you like **my / mine**?
2 Is this jacket **your / yours**?
3 Do you like **our / ours** house?
4 **Her / Hers** bike is better than his.
5 **Their / theirs** dog is very small.
6 **My / Mine** favourite hobby is playing the guitar.

Unit 12

○ Conjunctions *and*, *but*, *or*

His clothes are green **and** yellow.
I'm big **but** I'm not strong.
Are you tall **or** short?

1 Make sentences.

1 A zebra is a fast runner
2 A horse doesn't eat meat
3 A frog can be green, yellow, blue

A but it eats grass.
B or orange.
C and it's black and white.

2 Write *and*, *but* or *or*.

1 The lizard is small _____ green.
2 Tigers are scary _____ I like them.
3 It's a small butterfly _____ it's beautiful.
4 My cat is black _____ white.
5 Eva likes football _____ tennis.
6 Monsters can be happy _____ angry.
7 I'm not thirsty _____ I'm hungry.
8 Would you like an orange juice _____ an apple juice?

75

Grammar fun pairwork!

Unit 7

○ *Would like + noun or verb*

1 What would you like? Ask and answer with a friend.

a drink	talk to a robot
a crocodile	have a pet
a duck	sing a song
a motorbike	go to a zoo
a kite	ride a horse

Examples
– Would you like a drink?
– Yes, I would.
– Would you like to talk to a robot?
– No, I wouldn't.

Unit 1

○ Question words *what, how, who, how many*

Student A

2 Ask a friend questions about Eva. Use *what colour*, *how*, *how many* and *who*. Write the answers.

Example
A: What's her name?
B: Her name's Eva.

Name:	Sam
Eye colour:	blue
Brothers:	2
Sisters:	1
Best friend:	Anna
Goes to school:	by bus

Name:	Eva
Eye colour:	___
Brothers:	___
Sisters:	___
Best friend:	___
Goes to school:	___

Unit 3

○ Question word *where* & prepositions of place

Student A

3 Where are they? Ask a friend questions. Draw.

Listen to your friend and answer. Ask about:

| Piper |
| Frankie |
| Nedda |

Examples
B: Where is Piper?
A: He's in the garden. He's under the tree.

Units 5 and 10

○ Determiners: *a, the, some*
Nouns: countable and uncountable

Student A

5 Tell a friend about the food.

Listen to your friend and draw.

Examples
A: There's some orange juice.

Grammar fun pairwork!

Unit 12

○ Conjunctions *and*, *but*, *or*

2 Add the conjunctions with a friend.

1 She's a good runner she can't swim.

_____

2 He drinks orange juice apple juice for breakfast.

_____

3 They like bears hippos.

_____

Unit 1

○ Question words *what*, *how*, *who*, *how many*

Student B

3 Ask a friend questions about Sam. Use *what colour*, *how*, *how many* and *who*. Write the answers.

Examples B: *What's his name?*
A: *His name's Sam.*

Name:	Sam
Eye colour:	_____
Brothers:	_____
Sisters:	_____
Best friend:	_____
Goes to school:	_____

Name:	Eva
Eye colour:	brown
Brothers:	1
Sisters:	1
Best friend:	Grace
Goes to school:	by car

Unit 3

○ Question word *where* & prepositions of place

Student B

4 Where are they? Ask a friend questions. Draw.

Listen to your friend and answer. Ask about:

| Max |
| Frankie |
| Nedda |

Examples A: *Where is Max?*
B: *He's in the bedroom. He's on the bed.*

Units 5 and 10

○ Determiners: *a*, *the*, *some*
Nouns: countable and uncountable

Student B

5 Tell a friend about the food.

Listen to a friend and draw.

Examples B: *There's some lemonade.*

Reading & Writing Checklist

Circle  if your answer is Yes!

My handwriting is clear and tidy.	
I don't have problems spelling English words.	
I can show if a word matches a picture by drawing a tick or a cross.	
I know and can spell more than five food words.	
I can answer questions about a picture with 'yes' or 'no'.	
I can understand a short story with pictures.	
I know and can spell more than five words for things at the beach.	
I can write sentences about what people are doing.	
I know and can spell more than five words for things in the house.	
I can answer questions about a story by filling in gaps.	
I knew the words for all the things in Max's school bag in task 3 on page 7.	

I knew all the words in task 5 on page 9 and ticked and crossed the boxes correctly.

I wrote the sentences about the children in the park correctly in task 6 on page 11.

I wrote about me and my friend in task 4 on page 18.

I read the instructions and made a pop-up card in task 7 on page 19.

I unjumbled the words for places you see numbers in task 4 on page 29.

I wrote the correct words in the gaps in the text about frogs in task 4 on page 33.

I remember the six adjectives in task 3 on page 42 and I can spell them.

I wrote six sentences about the crocodile in task 4 on page 47.

I matched the sentences about the children on a school trip to the correct pictures in task 6 on page 57.

How many magic squirrels did you get?

Listening Checklist

Circle  if your answer is Yes!

 I can recognise lots of words I know when they are spoken in my book.

 I matched the names to the correct school bags in task 2 on page 6.

 I like matching names to a picture of people by drawing a line.

 I circled the correct answers about the alien in task 4 on page 23.

 I can understand and write the numbers 1–20 when I hear them.

 I pointed to the correct pictures of children in the house in task 6 on page 31.

 I can choose the correct picture when I hear it described.

 I put the pictures of the children in a café in the correct order in task 2 on page 38.

 I can colour a picture when I listen to a description.

 I circled the pictures with the correct colour in task 2 on page 64.

How many magic squirrels did you get?

Speaking Checklist

Check your progress, colour the stars!   OK   Great

Statement	OK	Great
I can understand questions my teacher asks in English.	☆	☆☆
I asked and answered questions about what is in a school bag in task 5 on page 7.	☆	☆☆
I can talk about a picture using sentences, not just one word.	☆	☆☆
I talked with my friend about what we do on our birthdays in task 2 on page 16.	☆	☆☆
I can answer questions about pictures with short answers.	☆	☆☆
I described my tree house in task 3 on page 30.	☆	☆☆
I enjoyed acting out ordering a meal in a café in task 5 on page 39.	☆	☆☆
I can speak about myself and what I like doing.	☆	☆☆
I talked about the things I take to the beach in task 3 on page 52.	☆	☆☆
It's fun to speak English in class.	☆	☆☆

Word list

Unit 1
bag n ___
blue adj ___
classroom n ___
colour n ___
crayon n ___
cupboard n ___
desk n ___
draw v ___
green adj ___
pen n ___
photo n ___
pink adj ___
poster n ___
purple adj ___
read v ___
ruler n ___
school n ___
talk v ___
write v ___
yellow adj ___

Unit 2
ball n ___
bat n ___
bike n ___
bird n ___

boat n ___
boots n ___
brown adj ___
camera n ___
catch v ___
clean adj ___
crocodile n ___
dirty adj ___
dog n ___
duck n ___
eat v ___
fish n ___
flower n ___
football n ___
handbag n ___
hit v ___
hold v ___
ice cream n ___
kick v ___
kite n ___
monkey n ___
paper n ___
park n ___
pick up v ___
picture n ___
ride v ___
run v ___

skateboard n _____
sleep v _____
snake n _____
sun n _____
throw v _____
walk v _____
water n _____

Unit 3
balloon n _____
birthday n _____
cake n _____
chair n _____
clothes n _____
open v _____
robot n _____
sing v _____
song n _____
toy n _____

Unit 4
alien n _____
beach n _____
bear n _____
bed n _____
bedroom n _____
black adj _____
board game n _____
book n _____

bread n _____
burger n _____
ear n _____
face n _____
foot/feet n _____
frog n _____
giraffe n _____
goat n _____
grape n _____
happy adj _____
horse n _____
lemon n _____
lemonade n _____
lizard n _____
mango n _____
monster n _____
onion n _____
orange adj _____
paint v _____
pea n _____
pear n _____
pineapple n _____
plane n _____
playground n _____
sad adj _____
sand n _____
sea n _____

83

shop n _____

skateboarding n _____

smile n _____

spider n _____

sweet(s) n _____

tail n _____

train n _____

TV n _____

watermelon n _____

white adj _____

zoo n _____

Unit 5

banana n _____

bookshop n _____

bus n _____

chicken n _____

chocolate n _____

clock n _____

close v _____

computer n _____

doll n _____

door n _____

egg n _____

glasses n _____

grandma n _____

hat n _____

house n _____

jacket n _____

jeans n _____

kiwi n _____

lime n _____

meatballs n _____

nose n _____

pie n _____

potato n _____

sock n _____

street n _____

teacher n _____

teddy (bear) n _____

tomato n _____

T-shirt n _____

Unit 6

armchair n _____

bathroom n _____

dinner n _____

guitar n _____

jellyfish n _____

kitchen n _____

mirror n _____

piano n _____

polar bear n _____

scary adj _____

tree n _____

wall n _____

Unit 7
breakfast n _____
carrot n _____
coconut n _____
juice n _____
lunch n _____
orange n _____
rice n _____

Unit 8
baseball n _____
basketball n _____
cat n _____
clap v _____
sheep n _____
shorts n _____
tennis n _____
window n _____

Unit 9
elephant n _____
fly v _____
hippo n _____
jump v _____
shoe n _____
swim v _____
tiger n _____
zebra n _____

Unit 10
apple n _____
baseball cap n _____
shell n _____
ship n _____

Unit 11
car n _____
cow n _____
pencil n _____
phone n _____
sit v _____
tablet n _____
watch n _____

Unit 12
hand n _____
keyboard (computer) n _____
mouse (computer) n _____
sofa n _____

In your book ...

Nedda

Likes: puppies, videos, drawing, spaghetti, the moon, unicorns

Dislikes: sharks, lions, aliens, broccoli

Captain Zoom

Likes: sports, snow, skating, caves

Dislikes: water, dancing, umbrellas

Bobbie

Likes: carrot, music, eggs, apples, running, dancing, pears, grapes

Dislikes: candy, riding bikes, lettuce, oranges

Leon

Likes: friends, gum

Dislikes: blood, scary things

Piper

Likes: flying, reading stories

Dislikes: walking, hats, boots

Frankie

Likes: fashion, pink, bed, hugs

Dislikes: soup

... from kids around the world

Alejandra, 8

Hugo, 8

Julia, 8

Luíza, 7

Alan, 6

Anna, 7

Jesse

Likes: flying, burritos, spiders, dancing, red, eating

Dislikes: mushrooms, yellow, cats, black

Checklist buddy

Likes: pizza, apple juice, playing ball

Dislikes: ice cream, burgers, mice, cats

Exam Professor

Likes: science, music, interesting animals, playing basketball

Dislikes: disorder, meat, destruction, black

Max

Likes: balloons, bananas, apples

Dislikes: cleaning my room

Think Big Giraffe

Likes: plants

Dislikes: meat

Sage

Likes: reading, eating, joking, art

Dislikes: pickles, flies, the dark, cockroaches

Aurora, 9

Luisa, 7

Mariya, 8

Mario, 11

Adriana, 7

Edith, 11

Author acknowledgements

Claire Medwell would like to give thanks to the editorial team for all their help and support throughout the writing process and to her children who provide an endless source of inspiration. She would also like to give special thanks to Matthew English from IH Reggio Calabria, Italy for his inspiring ideas on using Art in the YL's classroom.

Montse Watkin would like to acknowledge all the inspiring colleagues she has had the pleasure of working with over the years.

Publisher acknowledgements

The authors and publishers are grateful to the following for reviewing the material during the writing process:

Jane Ritter, Georgia Forte: Italy; Angela McFarland: Vietnam; Maritza Suarez Gonzalez: Mexico; Muruvvet Celik: Turkey; Roisin O'Farrell: Spain.

Acknowledgements

The authors and publishers acknowledge the following sources of copyright material and are grateful for the permissions granted. While every effort has been made, it has not always been possible to identify the sources of all the material used, or to trace all copyright holders. If any omissions are brought to our notice, we will be happy to include the appropriate acknowledgements on reprinting & in the next update to the digital edition, as applicable.

Key: GR: Grammar; Rev: Review unit; U: Unit

Photography

All photographs are sourced from Getty Images.

GR: Jamie Grill/The Image Bank; Seseg Zhigzhitova/EyeEm; Philippe Desnerck/Photolibrary; Esther Moreno Martinez/EyeEm; PeopleImages/E+; Vadmary/iStock/Getty Images Plus; GILKIS - Emielke van Wyk/GILKIS - Emielke van Wyk; fmajor/iStock Unreleased; mediaphotos/iStock/Getty Images Plus; Rev: Jonas Gratzer/LightRocket; Creative Crop/DigitalVision; PhotoObjects.net/Getty Images Plus; PetrBonek/iStock/Getty Images Plus; Dan Thornberg/EyeEm; Ales-A/E+; Blend Images - Kris Timken; Brighton Dog Photography/Moment; Praveenkumar Palanichamy/Moment; Dorling Kindersley; Compassionate Eye Foundation/Rob Daly/OJO Images Ltd/Photodisc; Hero Images; Marc Romanelli; Asia Images Group; kupicoo/E+; SensorSpot/E+; Hill Street Studios/DigitalVision; Marcus Lyon/Photographer's Choice; Glow Images, Inc/Glow; fotosipsak/E+; Fuse/Corbis; kali9/E+; xefstock/E+; andresr/E+; Tang Ming Tung/Photodisc; **U1:** artisteer/iStock/Getty Images Plus; Will Heap/Dorling Kindersley; Stefano Cremisini/EyeEm; targovcom/iStock/Getty Images Plus; DAJ; Suparat Malipoom/EyeEm; epicurean/E+; HECTOR RETAMAL/AFP; Chau Doan/LightRocket; FatCamera/E+; Juanmonino/iStock/Getty Images Plus; Andersen Ross Photography Inc/DigitalVision; Juanmonino/E+; JohnnyGreig/E+; eskaylim/iStock/Getty Images Plus; Andy Crawford/Dorling Kindersley; **U2:** Glow Images; JGI/Jamie Grill; James O'Neil/DigitalVision; itsabreeze photography/Moment; DEA/L. ROMANO/De Agostini; **U3:** Mike Powell/Photodisc; Abhishek Thakur/EyeEm; Best View Stock; gpointstudio/iStock/Getty Images Plus; Colin Hawkins/Cultura; From Hurricane1984/Moment; PhotoAlto/Sigrid Olsson/PhotoAlto Agency RF Collections; Granger Wootz; Tang Ming Tung/Photodisc; **U4:** roevin/Moment; Stephen Oliver/Dorling Kindersley; Sharon White/Photographer's Choice; Dorling Kindersley: Charlotte Tolhurst; Yevgen Romanenko/Moment; Ronald Leunis/EyeEm; Jose A. Bernat Bacete/Moment; JohnnyGreig/E+; Maximilian Stock Ltd./Photolibrary; Paul Biris/Moment Open; Erich Karnberger/iStock/Getty Images Plus; devolmon/iStock/Getty Images Plus; Steve Debenport/E+; **U5:** Ng Sok Lian/EyeEm; Andy Crawford/Dorling Kindersley; Photo credit John Dreyer/Moment Open; Fotonen/iStock/Getty Images Plus; Yevgen Romanenko/Moment; Gary Ombler and Andy Crawford/Dorling Kindersley; Olga Gillmeister/iStock/Getty Images Plus; DustyPixel/E+; SabrinaPintus/iStock/Getty Images Plus; AleksandarGeorgiev/E+; Alexandre Macieira/EyeEm; lovelypeace/iStock/Getty Images Plus; Tom Craig/Photolibrary; Thomas Kline/Design Pics/Perspectives; Enes Evren/iStock/Getty Images Plus; chas53/iStock/Getty Images Plus; Anadolu Agency; Isabel Pavia/Moment Open; Esthermm/Moment; MoreISO/iStock Editorial/Getty Images Plus; michaelpuche/iStock/Getty Images Plus; Vstock LLC/VStock; Jessica Nelson/Moment Open; peepo/E+; **U6:** romana chapman/Moment; © Hiya Images/Corbis; PeopleImages/iStock/Getty Images Plus; Rawpixel/iStock/Getty Images Plus; sl-f/iStock/Getty Images Plus; Ed Freeman/Stone; David Santiago Garcia/Aurora; Vicki Jauron, Babylon and Beyond Photography/Moment; U7: Lina Moiseienko/iStock/Getty Images Plus; Kondor83/iStock/Getty Images Plus; Jose A. Bernat Bacete/Moment; Adisak Lapwutirat/EyeEm; Kemi H Photography/Moment Open; kiankhoon/iStock/Getty Images Plus; Education Images/Universal Images Group; Hero Images; istetiana/Moment; **U8:** FatCamera/E+; GraphicaArtis/Archive Photos; DEA/G. DAGLI ORTI; Universal History Archive/Universal Images Group; Gearstd/iStock/Getty Images Plus; Classen Rafael/EyeEm; Photo 12/Universal Images Group; U9: DLILLC/Corbis/VCG/Corbis Documentary; Richard Wager/Moment; The world is a beautiful place, there's beauty in everything/Moment; Paul Starosta/Corbis Documentary; Darrell Gulin/Photographer's Choice; Jose A. Bernat Bacete/Moment; Barcroft Media; ullstein bild; Ole Jorgen Liodden/naturepl.com/Nature Picture Library; Douglas Sacha/Moment; Martin Harvey/Gallo Images; JGI/Jamie Grill; **U10:** Charriau Pierre/The Image Bank; Stephen Knowles Photography/Moment; roevin/Moment; Westend61; Sergei Malgavko/TASS; joingate/iStock/Getty Images Plus; Dan Prince/Cultura; Arterra/Universal Images Group; **U11:** Westend61; Leland Bobbe/DigitalVision; andresr/E+; FatCamera/E+; xefstock/E+; Fotoatelier Berlin/imageBROKER; Yvette Cardozo/The Image Bank; kali9/iStock/Getty Images Plus; THEPALMER/E+; Mike Tauber; Meg Takamura; Marcy Maloy/Photodisc; **U12:** Shin Taro/Moment; PeopleImages/E+; Portra Images/Taxi; Wavebreakmedia/iStock/Getty Images Plus; Ariel Skelley/DigitalVision; Jose Luis Pelaez Inc/DigitalVision; Emrah Turudu/Photographer's Choice RF.

The following photograph is sourced from another library.
U8: Keith Haring artwork and writing © Keith Haring Foundation

Illustrations

Pablo Gallego (Beehive); Dave Williams (Bright); Leo Trinidad (Bright); Fran Brylewska (Beehive); Amanda Enright (Advocate); Collaborate Agency, Wild Apple Design Ltd.

Front cover illustrations by Amanda Enright; Leo Trinidad; Jhonny Nunez; Pol Cunyat; Benedetta Capriotti; Dan Widdowson; Pand P Studio/Shutterstock; Piotr Urakau/Shutterstock.

Audio

Audio production by Ian Harker

Song and chants composition and production by AmyJo Doherty and Martin Spangle.

Design

Design and typeset by Wild Apple Design Ltd
Cover design by Collaborate agency
Additional design layout EMC design Ltd